Blacktip Reef Sharks

by Grace Hansen

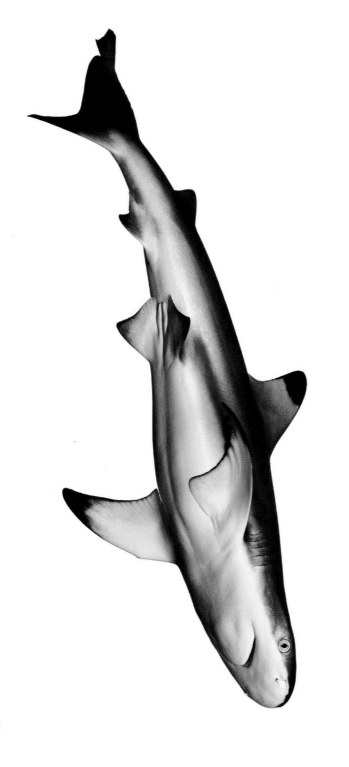

St. John the Baptist Parish Library
2920 Highway 51
LaPlace, LA 70068

Abdo
SHARKS
Kids

abdopublishing.com

Published by Abdo Kids, a division of ABDO, PO Box 398166, Minneapolis, Minnesota 55439.

Printed in the United States of America, North Mankato, Minnesota.

102015
012016

THIS BOOK CONTAINS
RECYCLED MATERIALS

Photo Credits: Animals Animals, iStock, Seapics.com, Shutterstock, Thinkstock

Production Contributors: Teddy Borth, Jennie Forsberg, Grace Hansen

Design Contributors: Laura Rask, Dorothy Toth

Library of Congress Control Number: 2015941989

Cataloging-in-Publication Data

Hansen, Grace.

Blacktip reef sharks / Grace Hansen.

p. cm. -- (Sharks)

ISBN 978-1-68080-150-7 (lib. bdg.)

Includes index.

1. Blacktip shark--Juvenile literature. I. Title.

597.3/4--dc23

2015941989

Table of Contents

Blacktip Reef Sharks

Blacktip reef sharks live in warm ocean waters. They live in bays and coral reefs near coasts.

The blacktip reef shark has large eyes. It has a short round nose.

At first glance, it looks like other sharks. The top half of its body is gray. The bottom half is white.

But this shark has some special features! It has black **markings** on the tips of its fins. It has white lines on its sides.

Food & Hunting

Blacktip reef sharks have rows of sharp teeth. Their teeth are great for catching prey.

These sharks like to eat reef fish. They also eat squid and other animals.

Blacktip reef sharks often hunt alone. They sometimes hunt in small groups.

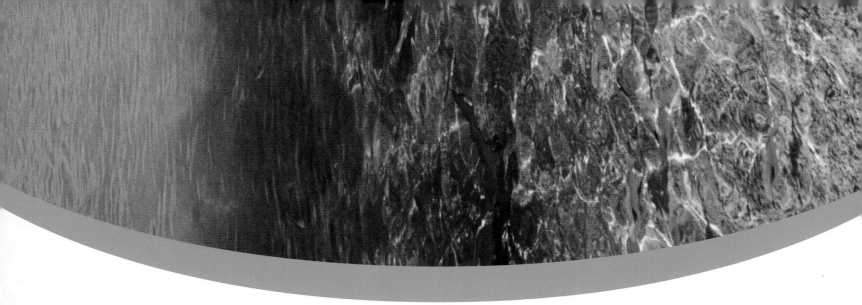

Baby Blacktip Reef Sharks

Baby sharks are called pups.

Blacktip reef sharks give

birth to 4 to 10 pups.

18

19

Pups are on their own right away. They swim near shorelines until they are stronger.

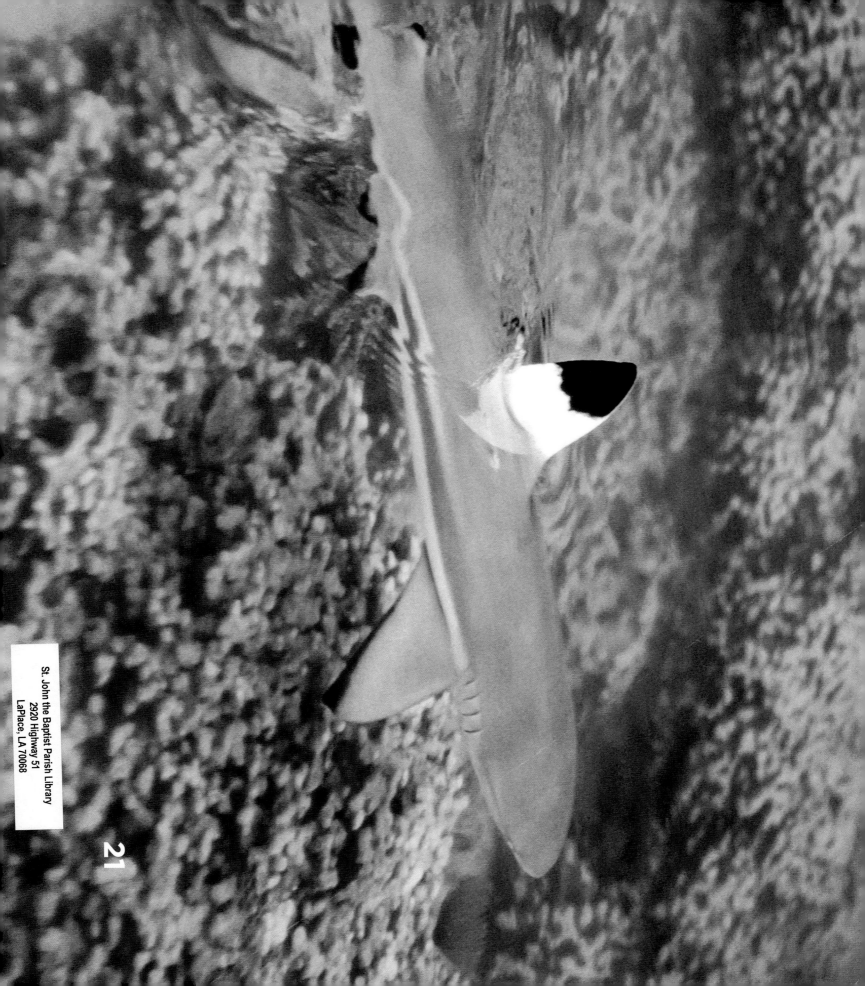

More Facts

- Blacktip reef sharks are sometimes found in freshwater.

- The blacktip reef shark is a good hunter. It chases schools of fish to shallow water. It is easier to catch them there.

- Blacktips are one of the most common sharks found near coral reefs.

Glossary

markings – a mark or pattern of marks on an animal's fur, feathers, or skin.

pup – a newborn animal.

reef fish – fish that are often found living near coral reefs.

shoreline – where water meets land.

Index

abdokids.com

Use this code to log on to abdokids.com and access crafts, games, videos, and more!

Abdo Kids Code:
SBK1507